TOUGH TRUCKS

GMC™ TRUCKS

BY SETH LYNCH

Gareth Stevens PUBLISHING

HOT TOPICS

Please visit our website, www.garethstevens.com. For a free color catalog of all our high-quality books, call toll free 1-800-542-2595 or fax 1-877-542-2596.

Cataloging-in-Publication Data
Names: Lynch, Seth.
Title: GMC trucks / Seth Lynch.
Description: New York : Gareth Stevens Publishing, 2019. | Series: Tough trucks | Includes glossary and index.
Identifiers: LCCN ISBN 9781538231586 (pbk.) | ISBN 9781538230336 (library bound) | ISBN 9781538231593 (6 pack)
Subjects: LCSH: Trucks--Juvenile literature. | General Motors Corporation--Juvenile literature.
Classification: LCC TL230.15 L96 2019 | DDC 629.224--dc23

Published in 2019 by
Gareth Stevens Publishing
111 East 14th Street, Suite 349
New York, NY 10003

Designer: Katelyn E. Reynolds
Editor: Kristen Nelson

Photo credits: Cover, p. 1 Leonard Zhukovsky/Shutterstock.com; cover, pp. 1–32 (background) phiseksit/Shutterstock.com; p. 5 betto rodrigues/Shutterstock.com; p. 7 Infrogmation/Wikipedia.org; pp. 8, 13, 30 (1960s) Underwood Archives/Getty Images; p. 9 Buyenlarge/Getty Images; p. 11 George Rodger/The LIFE Picture Collection/Getty Images; p. 14 Bob C/Shutterstock.com; p. 15 Chevrolet pre-1978/Tony Patt/Wikipedia.org; pp. 17, 30 (1990s Sierra) Jacobbell9/Shutterstock.com; pp. 19, 30 (1990s Sonoma) Car Culture, Inc./Car Culture® Collection/Getty Images; pp. 21, 30 (2000s Sierra) HumanZoom/Wikipedia.org; pp. 23, 30 (2000s Canyon) Sfoskett~commonswiki/Wikipedia.org; pp. 25, 30 (2017) Ed Aldridge/Shutterstock.com; pp. 27, 29 Raymond Boyd/Getty Images; pp. 28, 30 (2018) Steve Lagreca/Shutterstock.com.

Printed in the United States of America

CPSIA compliance information: Batch #CW19GS: For further information contact Gareth Stevens, New York, New York at 1-800-542-2595.

CONTENTS

MANY TRUCKS

From small to heavy-duty, GMC has been making pickup trucks of all sizes for more than 100 years. Today, the GMC Sierra and the GMC Canyon are some of the best-selling trucks on the road.

FULL THROTTLE!

A pickup truck has a closed cab where the driver sits. It has an open back that has low sides, which is often used for **hauling**. Heavy-duty pickups are larger and can haul more.

TRUCK COMPANY

The General Motors Truck Company—today called GMC—began when General Motors bought the Rapid Motor **Vehicle** Company in 1909. The first GMC trucks were shown at the New York Auto Show in 1912.

GMC TRUCKS

GMC Quality Its Own Best Proof

When a product is built inherently good—good for its own sake—that fact will inevitably impress itself upon the minds of users and prospective users.

This is on the principle that truth will prevail. And this is the principle underlying the rapidly widening reputation of GMC trucks for plain, honest quality.

No motor truck can establish for itself lasting confidence unless its quality is proved by use. No business can become truly great and permanent unless founded on a sound and legitimate basis.

So GMC trucks are fast reaping the benefits of true quality—that genuineness of merit which reflects the high ideals of the builders.

GMC quality is fighting its own battle against every approach of inferiority.

GMC trucks are not only good, but able to prove it in performance.

That users keep on buying more GMC trucks is evidence of this fact.

Let your next truck be a GMC.

GENERAL MOTORS TRUCK COMPANY
Pontiac, Michigan
Branches and Distributors in Principal Cities

(492)

GMC TRUCKS

Mention The Geographic—It

FULL THROTTLE!

Before becoming part of GM, the Rapid Motor Vehicle Company was making commercial trucks, or those used by companies buying and selling goods.

During the 1920s, the **design** of GMC trucks began to take shape. By the 1930s, more paint colors and room in the cab for passengers were added. This made more people want to buy a pickup!

GMC plant, 1920s

FULL THROTTLE!

For many years, Chevrolet and GMC trucks have been made in the same factories and with the same parts. In the 2000s, GMCs started to have more of their own look.

DUCKS IN A WAR

GMC was a big part of the war effort during World War II (1939–1945). They made hundreds of thousands of trucks for the US Army and the **Allies**. One kind called the "duck" was amphibious, meaning it could be driven on land or in water!

DUKW

FULL THROTTLE!

General Dwight D. Eisenhower said the GMC DUKW, or duck, was one of the machines that helped the Allies win the war.

GETTING MODERN

From the 1950s to the 1970s, GMC worked to make their truck designs better. They wanted to improve drivers' comfort, how much the trucks could haul, and the look of their trucks. GMC was making **interiors** comfortable for passengers, too!

1967 GMC pickup

FULL THROTTLE!

During the Korean War (1950–1953), GMC made more than 9,000 military vehicles for the US forces.

In 1971, GMC introduced a light pickup called the Sprint. It was supposed to give buyers a choice between trucks made to haul and cars. It looked sportier than other trucks GMC made. In 1978, the Sprint's name was changed to the Caballero.

Sprint

Chevy El Camino

FULL THROTTLE!

The Sprint was built based on the design of the Chevy El Camino!

THE FULL-SIZE SIERRA

GMC made trucks called Sierra starting in 1962. In 1988, the company made Sierra the name for all their full-size pickup trucks. The 1988 Sierra 1500 and Sierra 2500 were available with a **V6 engine**. The Sierra 3500 had a more powerful engine!

FULL THROTTLE!

The Chevrolet Silverado has looked almost exactly like the GMC Sierra, both inside and out, since the beginning!

THE SMALL SONOMA

In 1991, GMC updated their small pickup and called it the Sonoma. They also introduced a **version** of the Sonoma called the GMC Syclone. This high-performance truck could go from standing still to 60 miles (97 km) per hour in about 5 seconds!

1992 Sonoma

FULL THROTTLE!

In 1996, GMC Truck changed their name officially to just GMC.

A NEW SIERRA

The 1999 GMC Sierra was better than ever. It had a 200-**horsepower**, V8 engine. The Sierra Classic 1500 could tow up to 7,000 pounds (3,175 kg) and could haul more than 2,000 pounds (907 kg)!

FULL THROTTLE!

A third door was added to the Sierra's cab in the 1990s to make it easier for passengers to climb into the truck.

CANYON DEBUT

The GMC Canyon came out in 2004 to replace the Sonoma pickup. It had a powerful engine for its size and used fuel better than other trucks on the road at the time. GMC offered a Canyon with features especially for off-road driving, too!

FULL THROTTLE!

Many vehicles are made in different trim levels, or with different features, parts, or abilities. In 2007, GMC introduced **luxury** features in a trim level called Denali.

ON THE ROAD NOW!

Today, GMC's small pickup truck, the Canyon, comes in several trim levels including SLE, SLT, and Denali. The 2018 Canyon Denali had a 308-horsepower, V6 engine. It could reach 60 miles (97 km) per hour in less than 7 seconds!

2017 Canyon Denali

FULL THROTTLE!

The Denali trim level offers such fancy features as heated seats and the ability to charge a cellphone without a cord.

The GMC Sierra is still available as a light-duty pickup truck. But the Sierra HD offers even more towing and hauling ability. The 2018 Sierra 3500HD can tow up to 23,300 pounds (10,569 kg) and carry more than 7,000 pounds (3,175 kg)!

2017 Sierra Denali HD

FULL THROTTLE!

GMC has also made a Sierra built to drive well on- and off-road: the Sierra 1500 All Terrain X.

The Sierra 2500 Denali HD All Mountain truck has features that would make it the best truck for driving over snow and mud. It doesn't have tires—it has tracks like a bulldozer! This inventive vehicle shows what GMC can do with trucks in the future!

FULL THROTTLE!

The Sierra 2500 Denali HD All Mountain is a concept truck. That means it's not ready to be bought by the public yet!

GMC TRUCKS THROUGH HISTORY

1960s

Sonoma

1990s

Sierra

Sierra

2000s

Canyon

2017

Canyon

Sierra HD All Mountain

2018

FOR MORE INFORMATION

BOOKS

Less, Emma. *Mechanics*. Mankato, MN: Amicus Readers, Amicus Ink, 2018.

Weber, M. *Wild Moments of Truck Racing*. North Mankato, MN: Edge Books, Capstone Press, 2018.

WEBSITES

GMC

www.gmc.com

Check out the full lineup of trucks GMC has to offer.

Pickup Truck Buying Guide

www.consumerreports.org/cro/cars/pickup-trucks/buying-guide

Read all about the different features pickup trucks may have and how to compare them.

Publisher's note to educators and parents: Our editors have carefully reviewed these websites to ensure that they are suitable for students. Many websites change frequently, however, and we cannot guarantee that a site's future contents will continue to meet our high standards of quality and educational value. Be advised that students should be closely supervised whenever they access the internet.

GLOSSARY

Allies: the group of nations, including England and the United States, in World War II that opposed the Axis nations, including Germany and Japan

design: the pattern or shape of something

haul: to pull or carry something heavy

horsepower: a unit used to measure the power of an engine

interior: inside

luxury: something that offers more than needed and usually costs more

V6 engine: an engine, or machine that makes power, with two banks of three cylinders arranged in a V shape. A V8 engine has two banks for four cylinders arranged in a V shape.

vehicle: an object used for carrying or transporting people or goods, such as a car, truck, or airplane

version: a form of something that is different from others

INDEX